10 IMPROVISATIONAL ALTO SAX ETUDES
by Jeff Coffin

ISBN 9781953622068
Copyright © 2020 by Jeff Coffin. All rights reserved.
No part of this book may be duplicated or shared without the permission of Jeff Coffin.

Also available online as an e-book.
Special thanks to Josh Karas for his assistance.
Layout and cover design by Robert Hakalski.
Engraving by Kyle Gordon.
Back cover photo courtesy of Jeff Coffin.
www.jeffcoffin.com/sax

WELCOME!

What you have here are my *Ten Improvisational Alto Sax Etudes*. I originally played and then transcribed them on flute (available as *10 Improvisational Flute Etudes, 10 Improvisational Clarinet Etudes, 10 Improvisational Tenor Sax Etudes*) and they work great for alto sax too!

I have provided free MP3 streaming and downloads at www.jeffcoffin.com/sax so you can hear and get a feel for the solos. They are played by yours truly on alto.

If you want to play through them with backing tracks, which is best, I recommend getting the iRealPro app so you can change the various settings to your liking. If this is already a familiar musical language and style for you, choose your own tempo and just start playing. If not, please listen to the examples and try to imitate how the etudes are being played. I recommend taking them quite slowly at first and eventually build them up to an excruciatingly fast tempo that makes your key joints smoke from the friction!! Well, I DO recommend starting slowly.

These solo etudes are improvisations I played using iReal Pro. I recorded into Pro Tools, transcribed my solos (tip: get the rhythms first if you're writing down solos), made some edits, put them into Sibelius, fixed the errors I made putting them into Sibelius, re-recorded them with the corrections and edits, and now they are ready to be played. Easy! :-)

I chose the chord changes to standard jazz repertoire that I thought would be familiar, beneficial, and fun to play. I think this book has something for everyone. Oh, and I named the solos just for fun.

Some of these might be pretty challenging but it's always good to have things to work on that take some extra effort. I wouldn't want you to be bored.

The recorded tempos are for example only so it doesn't matter if you play them slower to faster than the recording when you're playing them on your own. Find tempos that work for you and that allow you to sound good and execute the material.

I hope you have a fun time with these and that you learn some things along the way. I know I did. Good luck!

Peace, JC

jeffcoffin444@gmail.com
www.jeffcoffin.com/sax

TABLE OF CONTENTS

4-6 **Olive Mi** = All of Me
7 **Space Flies Like Star Pies** = Star Eyes
8-11 **Bluetude** = Blues (B♭ & C concert)
12-13 **It's The Little Things** = All The Things You Are
14-15 **Mrs. Kowalski** = Stella By Starlight
16-17 **The Answer Is Yes!** = Confirmation
18-20 **The Jones Tones** = Have You Met Miss Jones
22-23 **It's Only You** = There Will Never Be Another You
24-25 **King Of Leaps** = Giant Steps
26-27 **Where My Photos At?** = Someday My Prince Will Come

I dug the way Jeff Coffin has put this book of 10 of his improvisations on some famous music together. His melodic ideas will give way for you to develop your own. Learn the tunes and have some fun!!

Joe Lovano / Saxophonist
(Grammy Winner, Composer, ECM Recording Artist, Gary Burton Chair in Jazz Performance,
Berklee College of Music)

Jeff Coffin put together a very unique set of improvisations based on the changes of some classic jazz standards. He presents it in a way that allows the player to hear the chords of the songs behind the improvisations. Being a great saxophone player himself, with this book he is able to increase anyones jazz vocabulary just by playing thru them! Well done Jeff!

Bill Evans / Saxophonist
(Miles Davis, Herbie Hancock, John McLaughlin, Mick Jagger)

In this new collection of études my friend Jeff Coffin blesses us with a brilliant batch of bite-sized morsels to be digested into our "system" of improvisation. Fact is, every complex thing is an aggregate (and most times faster) version of lots of simpler, slower things. Much like vocabulary, Jeff helps prepare us for better, more meaningful, cogent, deeper musical conversations by giving us a more facile way of breaking things down.

Kirk Whalum / Saxophonist
(Grammy Winner, Whitney Houston, Bob James, Quincy Jones, Luther Vandross)

OLIVE MI
All of Me

Comp. **Jeff Coffin**

SPACE FLIES LIKE STAR PIES
Star Eyes

Comp. **Jeff Coffin**

BLUETUDE
Blues in G

Comp. **Jeff Coffin**

BLUETUDE

BLUETUDE
Blues in A

Comp. **Jeff Coffin**

BLUETUDE

IT'S THE LITTLE THINGS

All The Things You Are

Comp. **Jeff Coffin**

IT'S THE LITTLE THINGS

MRS. KOWALSKI
Stella By Starlight

Comp. **Jeff Coffin**

MRS. KOWALSKI

THE ANSWER IS YES!
Confirmation

Comp. **Jeff Coffin**

THE ANSWER IS YES!

fine

THE JONES TONES
Have You Met Miss Jones

Comp. **Jeff Coffin**

THE JONES TONES

THE JONES TONES

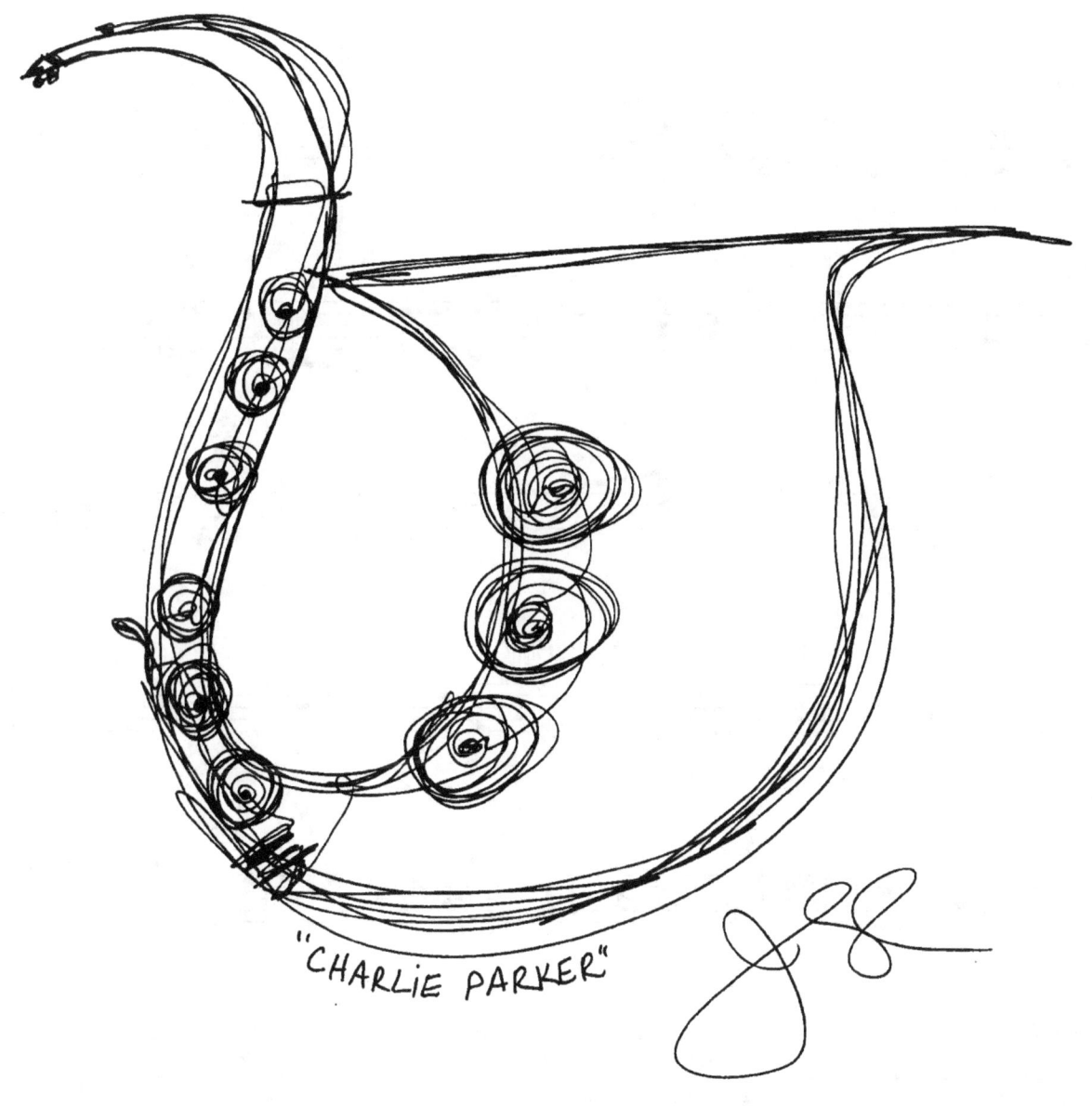
"CHARLIE PARKER"

IT'S ONLY YOU
There Will Never Be Another You

Comp. **Jeff Coffin**

-22-

IT'S ONLY YOU

KING OF LEAPS
Giant Steps

Comp. **Jeff Coffin**

-24-

KING OF LEAPS

WHERE MY PHOTOS AT?
Someday My Prince Will Come

Comp. **Jeff Coffin**

WHERE MY PHOTOS AT?

ALSO BY JEFF COFFIN

10 Improvisational Flute Etudes
10 Improvisational Clarinet Etudes
10 Improvisational Tenor Sax Etudes
The Road Book
The Saxophone Book (1-3)
Jeff Coffin & the Mu'tet Play-Along
The Articulate Jazz Musician (w/Caleb Chapman)

Available at www.jeffcoffin.com

www.ingramcontent.com/pod-product-compliance
Lightning Source LLC
Chambersburg PA
CBHW081312070526
44578CB00006B/851